To

From

Other books in this series:

HAPPY ANNIVERSARY

To someone special on the birth of
    A LOVELY NEW BABY

To a very special DAD

To a very special DAUGHTER

To a very special FRIEND

To a very special GRANDDAUGHTER

To a very special GRANDMA

To a very special GRANDPA

To a very special GRANDSON

Wishing you HAPPINESS

To my very special HUSBAND

Someone very special…
    TO THE ONE I LOVE

To a very special MOTHER

To a very special SISTER

To a very special SON

To a very special TEACHER

To my very special WIFE

Published in 1996 by Helen Exley Giftbooks in Great Britain.
This edition published in 2008

12 11 10 9 8 7 6 5 4 3 2 1

ISBN 13: 978-1-84634-300-1

Illustrations and design © Helen Exley 1996, 2008
Important copyright notice: Pam Brown, Charlotte Gray and Jenny De Vries are all
© Helen Exley 1996, 2008
The moral right of the author has been asserted.
A copy of the CIP data is available from the British Library on request.

Acknowledgements: The publishers are grateful for permission to reproduce
copyright material. While every effort has been made to trace copyright holders,
Exley Publications would be pleased to hear from any not here acknowledged:
Ogden Nash: The extracts "Love is to need…." and "An occasional lucky guess…."
and the extract from "Marriage Lines" are reprinted by permission of the publisher
Little, Brown & Co and Curtis Brown.
Printed in China.
'TO A VERY SPECIAL'® IS A REGISTERED TRADE MARK OF HELEN EXLEY GIFTBOOKS

Helen Exley Giftbooks, 16 Chalk Hill, Watford, Herts WD19 4BG, UK.
www.helenexleygiftbooks.com

Wishing you happiness
FOR YOUR WEDDING

ILLUSTRATIONS BY JULIETTE CLARKE.
EDITED BY HELEN EXLEY.

The greatest gift that I would wish for you
is empathy, the skill to see
into each other's minds and hearts
with love and understanding, and
to help each other to realize your dreams.

HELEN EXLEY®

A NEW LIFE

In the opinion of the world,
marriage ends all, as it does in a comedy.
The truth is precisely the opposite:
it begins all.

ANNE SOPHIE SWETCHINE

Marriage is a serious business,
but love turns the grey of life to gold.

MIRIAM OSBORNE

Marriage is the place
where you can at last be comfortable.
You can take off the too-tight shoes
and dress for comfort.

PAM BROWN, b.1928

A marriage makes of two fractional lines a whole;
it gives to two purposeless lives a work,
and doubles the strength of each to perform it;
it gives to two questioning natures a reason for
living, and something to live for.

MARK TWAIN (1835-1910)

Marriage sets mathematics on its head –
for at one swoop it halves all troubles.
Being shared, multiplies joys out of all reckoning,
divides responsibilities, doubles perception.

PAM BROWN, b.1928

That quiet mutual gaze of a trusting husband
and wife is like the first moment of rest
or refuge from a great weariness or a great danger.

GEORGE ELIOT (MARY ANN EVANS) (1819-1880)

TO YOUR HAPPY MARRIAGE

There is a certain ease in a happy marriage –
a certainty, a contentment, that lies beneath
all change. May the coming years bring you
ever closer. May they give you contentment
and adventure, astonishments and peace.

PAM BROWN, b.1928

May this marriage be wine with halvah,
honey dissolving in milk. This marriage be the
leaves and fruit of a date tree.
This marriage be women laughing together for
days on end. This marriage a sign for us to study.
This marriage, beauty. This marriage, a moon
in a light-blue sky. This marriage, this silence
fully mixed with spirit.

RUMI, WRITTEN FOR HIS SON'S WEDDING

May heaven grant you in all things your
heart's desire – husband, house and a happy
peaceful home. For there is nothing better
in this world than that a man and woman,
sharing the same ideas, keep house together.
It discomforts their enemies and makes the hearts
of their friends glad – but they themselves know
more about it than anyone.

HOMER (8TH CENTURY B.C.), FROM "THE ODYSSEY"

MY PROMISE TO YOU...

I add my breath to your breath
That our days may be long in the earth
That the days of our people may be long
That we may be one person
That we may finish our roads together

KERES INDIAN SONG

Whither thou goest, I will go;
and where thou lodgest, I will lodge;
thy people shall be my
people, and thy God my God.

RUTH 1:16

Come live with me, and be my love,
And we will some new pleasures prove
Of golden sands, and crystal brooks,
With silken lines, and silver hooks.

JOHN DONNE (1572-1631),
FROM "THE BAIT"

"ROMANCE"

I will make you brooches and toys for your delight
Of bird-song at morning and star-shine at night.
I will make a palace fit for you and me,
Of green days in forests and blue days at sea.

I will make my kitchen and you shall keep your room,
Where white flows the river and bright blows the broom,
And you shall wash your linen and keep your body white
In rainfall at morning and dewfall at night.

And this shall be for music when no one else is near,
The fine song for singing, the rare song to hear!
That only I remember, that only you admire,
Of the broad road that stretches and the roadside fire.

ROBERT LOUIS STEVENSON (1850-1894)

WEDDING DAY!

I don't think I had any concerns when
I was walking down the aisle. I was very happy.
It's the culmination of everyone's dream
to find a person you can love who loves you.

TIPPER GORE

Where would we be without weddings?
They flower in the bleakest landscape –
gifts of hope and courage, faith and love,
in a weary world.

CHARLOTTE GRAY, b.1937

May this day be perfect

– or as near as dammit so!

Don't worry if the bridal wreathe settles

at a slightly jaunty angle,

or a wisp of hair escapes it.

Don't worry if the car gets stuck in traffic

and the vicar seems to have a nasty cold.

Don't worry if the organ wheezes

and the pageboy wriggles

and the Best Man fumbles with the ring.

You see each other –

and all else blurs away to insignificance.

Later – you will remember,

and laugh together.

But now no triviality can penetrate.

Love transforms everything.

Even Aunt Mildred's hat.

PAM BROWN, b.1928

...I love thee with the breath,
Smiles, tears, of all my life! –

ELIZABETH BARRETT BROWNING (1806-1861)

Now we will feel no rain
for each of us will be shelter for the other.
Now we will feel no cold
for each of us will be warmth for the other.
Now there is no more loneliness
for each of us will be companion to the other.
There is only one life before us
and our seasons will be long and good.

FROM AN APACHE WEDDING BLESSING

It's all I have to bring to-day, –
This, and my heart beside, –
This, and my heart, and all the fields, –
And all the meadows wide. –
Be sure you count – should I forget, –
Some one the sum could tell –
This, and my heart, and all the Bees
Which in the Clover dwell.

EMILY DICKINSON (1830-1886)

Love me with thine hand stretched out
Freely – open-minded.

ELIZABETH BARRETT BROWNING (1806-1861)

ONLY LOVE

Falling in love is largely delusion
– two hearts translating reality to dream.
But love is reality itself
– accepting, cherishing, delighting in
the individual oddities that make
a man and woman what they are.

PAM BROWN, b.1928

To love is nothing. To be loved is something.
To love, and be loved, is everything.

T. TOLIS V.

Love alone is capable of uniting living
beings in such a way as to complete and
fulfil them, for it alone takes them
and joins them by what is deepest in themselves.

PIERRE TEILHARD DE CHARDIN (1881-1955)

Love is like a mine. You go deeper and
deeper. There are passages, caves, whole strata.
You discover entire geological eras.

CHRISTOPHER ISHERWOOD

Nothing in life is as good as the marriage
of true minds between man and woman.
As good? It is life itself.

PEARL BUCK (1892-1973)

The keystone to any marriage
is one word: "WE".

PAM BROWN, b.1928

Love, the magician,
knows this little trick whereby
two people walk in different directions
yet always remain side by side.

HUGH PRATHER

The entire sum of existence is the magic
of being needed by just one person.

V. PUTNAM

It takes a lot of courage to show
your dreams to someone else.

ERMA BOMBECK (1927-1996)

There shall be such a oneness
between you that when one weeps,
the other shall taste salt.

PROVERB

Love is that condition
in which the happiness of another person
is essential to your own.

ROBERT HEINLEIN

HANDLE WITH GREAT CARE

A marriage where not only esteem,
but passion is kept awake, is, I am convinced,
the most perfect state of
sublunary happiness: but it requires great care
to keep this tender plant alive.

FRANCES BROOKE

I would like to have engraved
inside every wedding band, "Be kind
to one another." This is the Golden Rule of
marriage and the secret of making love last
through the years.

RANDOLPH RAY

Every enduring marriage involves an unconditional
commitment to an imperfect person.

GARY SMALLEY, FROM "LOVE IS A DECISION"

In the consciousness of belonging together,
in the sense of constancy, resides the sanctity,
the beauty of matrimony, which helps us
to endure pain more easily, to enjoy happiness
doubly, and to give rise to the fullest and finest
development of our nature.

FANNY LEWALD (1811-1889)

Love is to need, and needing, to be needed.
It is the patient architect that builds
Misunderstandings into understanding;
The sunrise, and the waking sea it gilds;
The far new shore, and the precarious landing.

OGDEN NASH (1902-1971)

THOSE UPS AND DOWNS

An occasional lucky guess as to what makes
a wife tick is the best a man can hope for.
Even then, no sooner has he learned how
to cope with the tick than she tocks.

OGDEN NASH (1902-1971)

To keep your marriage brimming,
With love in the loving cup,
Whenever you're wrong, admit it:
Whenever you're right, shut up.

OGDEN NASH (1902-1971),
FROM "MARRIAGE LINES"

Now some people think it's jolly
for to lead a single life,
But I believe in marriage
and the comforts of a wife.
In fact you might have quarrels,
just an odd one now and then,
It's worth your while a-falling out
to make it up again.

ENGLISH FOLK SONG

The great secret of a successful marriage
is to treat all disasters as incidents and none
of the incidents as disasters.

HAROLD NICHOLSON

A happy marriage is the union of two
good forgivers.

RUTH BELL GRAHAM

UNITED

You can never be happily married
to another until you get a divorce
from yourself. Successful marriage
demands a certain death to self.

JERRY MCCANT

No strong marriage can be
founded on "We'll see how long
we can make it last,"
only on "We will make it last."

JENNY DE VRIES

"Spiritual surrender"
is intentional. It is the result
of the free and unencumbered
use of one's will.

GERALD G. MAY

In loving one another you will discover
not only the depth and breadth and height
of each other's being – but your own.

PAM BROWN, b.1928

Two persons who have chosen each other
out of all the species, with the design
to be each other's mutual comfort
and entertainment, have, in that action,
bound themselves to be good-humoured,
affable, discreet, forgiving, patient, and joyful,
with respect to each other's frailties
and perfections, to the end of their lives.

JOSEPH ADDISON (1672-1719)

None can be eternally united
who have not died for each other.

COVENTRY PATMORE (1823-1896),
FROM "THE RED, THE ROOT AND THE FLOWER"

FOREVER TOGETHER

Treasure the love you receive above all.
It will survive long after your gold and good
health have vanished.

OG MANDINO

...Love bears all things, believes
all things, hopes all things, endures all things.
Love never ends....

I CORINTHIANS 13:4-8

A happy marriage is a long conversation
that always seems too short.

ANDRE MAUROIS (1885-1967)

Therefore mercifully ordain that we
may become aged together.

FROM "THE BOOK OF TOBIT"

FOR LIFE

Here begin the astonishments!
For you have only just begun
to know each other.
May this be a journey of wonder,
laughter, sympathy and kind companionship.

JENNY DE VRIES

It is a lovely thing to have a husband
and a wife developing together and having
the feeling of falling in love again.
That is what marriage really means.
Helping one another to reach the full status
of being persons, responsible and autonomous beings
who do not run away from life.

PAUL TOURNIER (1898-1986)

I think a man and a woman should choose each
other for life, for the simple reason that a long life
with all its accidents is barely enough for a man
and a woman to understand each other;
and in this case to understand is to love.

JOHN BUTLER YEATS (1839-1922)

Take hands – look into each other's eyes.
Each year you will discover more of one another
– and love more deeply.

PAM BROWN, b.1928